Dav........**......manton**

HarperCollins*Publishers*

keep
clear
To summon the four horsemen of the apocalypse please pull string provided.

CLEAR YOUR CONSCIENCE SWITCH.

OUT OF ORDER

BLOW DOORS OFF CLOWN'S CAR IN HUNGARIAN CIRCUS.

YES NO

300
HARROW GREEN GROUP
Name CLOWN
Location TOP SHELF
Position PRECARIOUSLY BALANCED
Comments
Label Colour: Red
0845 071 7777
www.harrowgreen.com

DRAGON'S HAY

FOR DRAGON'S USE ONLY

35

Brighton & Hove

CLICK HEELS THREE TIMES BEFORE PRESSING BUTTON

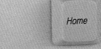

Home

Approximate minutes past each hour from this st...

	27A/27C	27B	29	35	27	27A	3
-Fri	Mon-Fri	Mon-Fri	Mon-Fri	Mon-Fri	Saturday	Saturday	Sat
dene	Hangleton and Mile Oak	Westdene	Shoreham Beach	Westdene	Westdene	Hangleton and Mile Oak	Wes
						58	
	58				14 35	45	
59NX	45				33	13 50	
	13 50	00X			05 35	20 50	
	20 50				05 35	20 50	
							21

Pigeon dial.

ruffle feathers

shit on tourist   coo

land

take off   shit on tramp

Please give up this seat
if Frank needs it.

25

Do not disturb the clockwork owl while the train is in motion.

On finding that you are seated next to yourself please consult the psychiatric manual located in the guard's compartment.

Magic Walnut.
Penalty for improper use - gypsy curse.

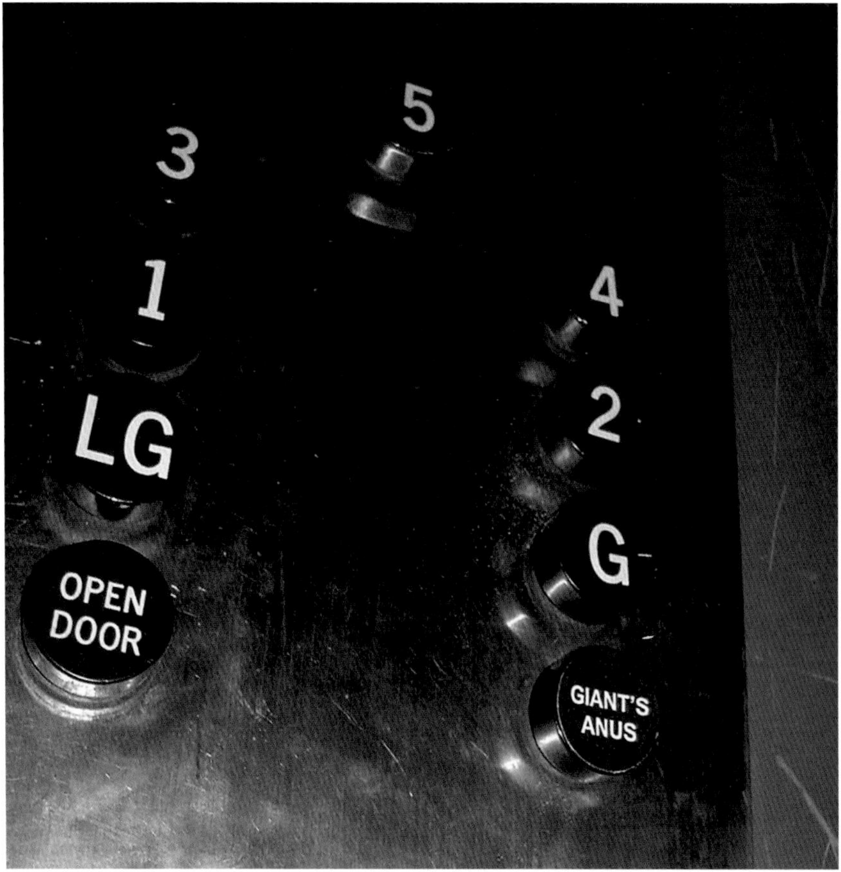
5
3
1
4
LG
2
G
OPEN DOOR
GIANT'S ANUS

Important notice:
All telephone conversations
will be recorded
by prying oddballs.

WARNING

Your pin number may be used by a Mr. Phil Oddmod to empty your bank account, thus enabling him to fund the astronomical maintenance costs of running his airship from where he is currently observing you through an extremely powerful telescope, cackling hysterically.

FLIES
QTY. 30
Compatible with DOGSHIT(model 17)
and WEDDING BUFFET(model 23)

Press button
to release truffle pigs.

In case of train delay please snap stresstwig.

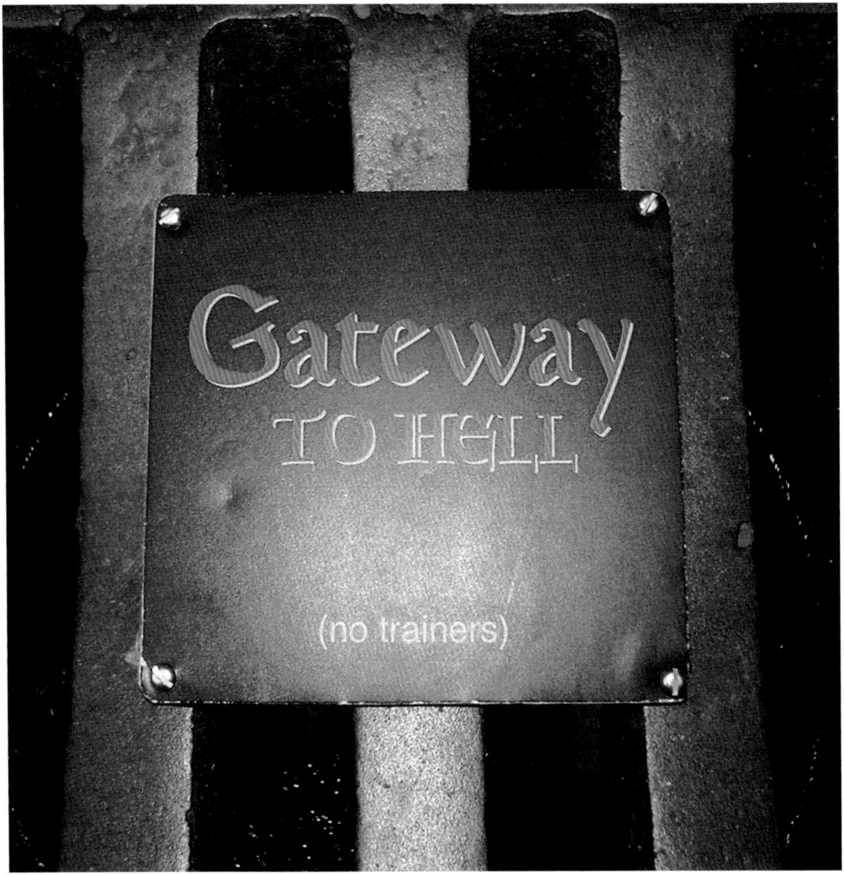
Gateway
TO HELL
(no trainers)

Warning. On opening this door you will find a darkened room. You will step inside and fumble for a light switch.

The door will slam behind you. You will be bundled to the ground and bitten on the ear.

By a monkey.

The lights will suddenly come on and mysteriously, the monkey will have disappeared. Along with one of your shoes.

CE

COMPLIES WITH EUROPEAN
SAFETY STANDARDS

Wallook Flownsh
All signs previously headed important notice are now headed Wallook Flownsh.

Emergency travel companion.

The British Institute
of false information

CAUTION

All your friends are paid for by the government.
Apart from Dave of course. He is, as you've
always suspected, a space-hornet from Jupiter.

CLOUD FORECAST

GENERALLY DULL THROUGHOUT THE MORNING.
IMPROVING THIS AFTERNOON WITH THE
APPEARANCE OF ONE LARGE GREY CLOUD SHAPED LIKE A CAT
FIRING SHOES FROM A BLUNDERBUSS.
THIS WILL LATER FRAGMENT INTO A SERIES OF SMALLER CLOUDS
ALL SHAPED LIKE NAPOLEON'S PICKLED COCK.

To avoid a lengthy prison sentence by injuring the knife wielding teenage thugs that will almost definitely accost you in this dodgy alleyway please defend yourself with this laughably ineffectual European Commission Approved Scary Hand.

TENNIS EQUIPMENT
HIRE CHARGES (PER HOUR)

RACKETS	£2.00
BALLS	£1.00
MUSICAL CLOGS	£5.00
BRONZE ONIONS	£3.00
MICE	£0.50
DYNAMITE	£3.00
STOVEPIPE HATS	£400.00

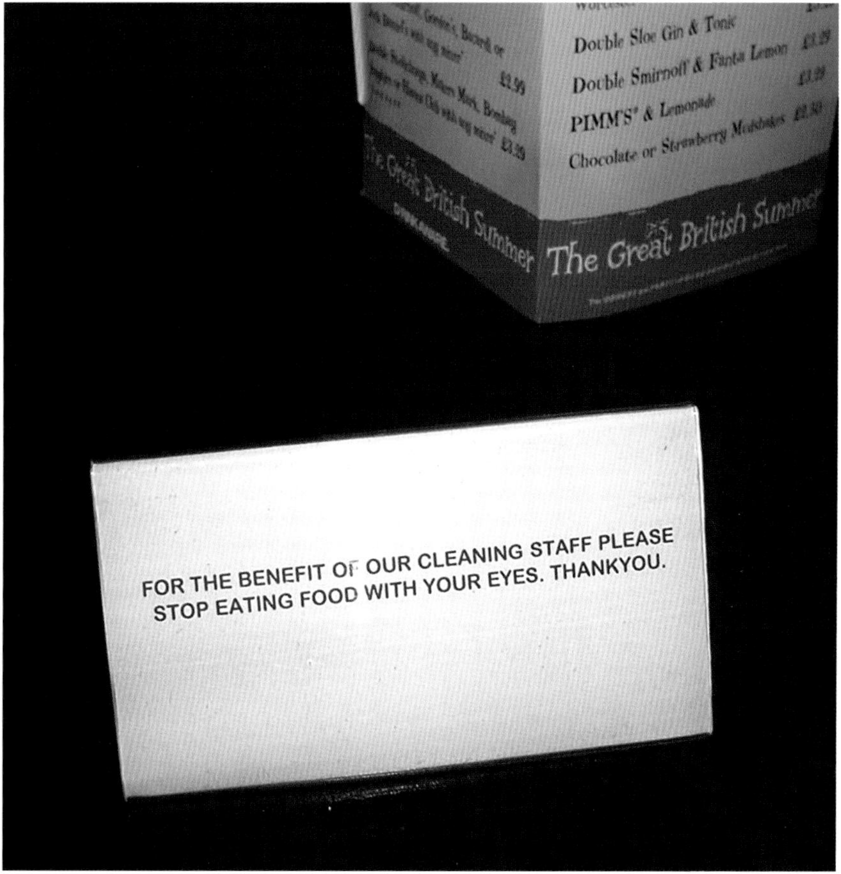

Double Sloe Gin & Tonic

Double Smirnoff & Fanta Lemon £3.29

PIMM'S & Lemonade

Chocolate or Strawberry Milkshakes £2.30

The Great British Summer

FOR THE BENEFIT OF OUR CLEANING STAFF PLEASE
STOP EATING FOOD WITH YOUR EYES. THANKYOU.

For a more efficient service, please alight at the next stop where a team of heavily drugged sloths will drag you to your destination.

Please ensure this glass is clean before taking your photograph

To achieve passport approved expression please follow instructions carefully.

1. *Adjust stool to a comfortable height.*
2. *Stare directly at camera.*
3. *Cast your mind back to that time you were alone in the house and you went to the kitchen to fetch the picnic eggs from the fridge and you tore off your shirt and feverishly smeared them around your nipples and you went to the bell jar and released the craneflies and it was good and you were weeping and you were laughing and you were weeping.*
4. *Insert coins.*

For Mum, Dad, Julie, Alfie and Barney. Love Dave.
For Mum, Dad, Sue, Bashful and Snuzzles. Love Alex.

HarperCollins*Entertainment*
An Imprint of HarperCollins*Publishers*
77–85 Fulham Palace Road,
Hammersmith, London W6 8JB

www.harpercollins.co.uk

Published by HarperCollins*Entertainment* 2005
1

A CIP catalogue record for this book
is available from the British Library

ISBN-13   978-0-00-721669-7
ISBN-10   0-00-721669-6

Printed and bound in Belgium by Proost NV, Turnhout